The Little Celebrations

Celebrating through the year in the Early Years Foundation Stage

Written by
Dawn Roper

Edited and introduced by Sally Featherstone

Illustrations by Martha Hardy

Little Books with **BIG**ideas®

The Little Book of Celebrations
ISBN 1-904187-59-5
978-1-904187-59-2

© Featherstone Education Ltd, 2007
Text © Dawn Roper, 2004
Illustrations © Martha Hardy, 2004
Series Editor, Sally Featherstone

First published in the UK, September 2004

'Little Books' is a trade mark of Featherstone Education Ltd

The right of Dawn Roper to be identified as the author of this work has been asserted in accordance with Sections 77 and 78 of the Copyright, Designs and Patents Act, 1988.

All rights reserved. No part of this publication may be reproduced by any means, stored in a retrieval system, or transmitted in any form or by any means, electronic, mechanical, photocopying, recording or otherwise, without the prior written consent of the publisher. This book may not be lent, sold, hired out or otherwise disposed of by way of trade in any form of binding or with any cover other than that in which it is published without the prior consent of the publisher, and without this condition being imposed upon the subsequent user.

Published 2008 by
A&C Black Publishers Limited
38 Soho Square, London W1D 3HB

To see our full range of titles visit **www.acblack.com**

Printed and Bound in the EU by Gutenberg Press Ltd, Malta

Contents

Focus of the page	page number
Introduction	4 and 5
Using the book	5
Links with the Early Learning Goals	6 and 7
A Celebrations Calendar	8 and 9
Who's New Round Here? (Christening; Christian)	10 and 11

Autumn Celebrations

Lanterns for Full Moon (Chinese Moon Festival)	12 and 13
Grandparents' Day	14 and 15
A Very Special Elephant (Ganesh Chathurthi Hindu)	16 and 17
Harvest Festival (European)	18 and 19
Firework Frenzy (5th November)	20 and 21
The Bonfire Band (5th November)	22 and 23
Wait for the New Moon (End of Ramadan; Muslim)	24 and 25
Light the Lights (Diwali; Hindu, Sikh)	26 and 27

Winter Celebrations

Light the Candles (Hannukkah; Jewish)	28 and 29
Waiting, waiting, waiting (St Nicholas; Christian)	30 and 31
The Special Baby (Christmas, the Nativity; Christian)	32 and 33
New Year Resolutions (New Year; Christian)	34 and 35
A Lucky Message in a Bag (Chinese New Year)	36 and 37
Dancing Dragons (Chinese New Year)	38 and 39

Spring Celebrations

Mix a Pancake (Shrove Tuesday; Christian)	40 and 41
Oh, Let's Have a Carnival (Mardi Gras; Caribbean)	42 and 43
Spray Day! (Holi; Hindu)	44 and 45
My Mum is the Best! (Mothering Sunday; Christian)	46 and 47
Spring into Springtime! (Spring)	48 and 49
Friends Together (Baisakhi; Sikh)	50 and 51
A Fruity Celebration (Passover; Jewish)	52 and 53
Easter Egg Hunt (Easter; Christian)	54 and 55
May Time (May Day)	56 and 57
Feed the Birds (Birth of Buddha; Buddhist)	58 and 59

Summer Celebrations

My Dad's Brilliant! (Father's Day)	60 and 61
Stars and Stripes (Fourth of July)	62 and 63

Any Season Celebrations

Brides and Grooms (Weddings)	64 and 65
Happy Birthday (Birthdays)	66 and 67
A Place to Worship (Visiting places of worship)	68 and 69
Appendix	70

Introduction

Living and working in a multicultural, multi-faith society offers many pleasures, and one of these is the opportunity to join in the celebrations of other faith and cultural groups. Although the curriculum in the UK is based in a Christian history and culture, the rich range of other cultures, faiths, societies and religions are valued and included by all who work in educational settings. They provide many opportunities for young children to learn about others, to appreciate other points of view and ways of doing things, to enjoy the colour of clothing, the flavours of food, the sounds of music, song and story.

As we put this book together, we have become aware of the ever widening range of cultural and faith groups arriving in settings as refugees, immigrants or temporary visitors. This adds to the opportunities and challenges of cultural inclusion, and has tested our choice of activities and celebrations. Of course we would like to be able to include the celebrations of every group, whatever their size, but we have limited space in one book, and have had to make a selection which we hope will be useful to all practitioners, wherever their setting is located.

We are also aware of the many faith and cultural groups that are, at present, in a minority in our country. These include Rastafarian, Baha'i, Jain, Shinto, and an increasing range of Christian groups, from Russian and Greek Orthodoxy to interpretations of traditional Christian denominations in the Caribbean and America. Unfortunately it was not possible to include the celebrations of all these groups in one book.

It is also important to recognise that some children grow up in virtual monocultures - in remote rural areas, in all white suburbs, in areas of high ethnic density in inner cities. These children have a right to access and understanding of other cultures and faiths, and to celebrate with enjoyment the wide range of festivals and special days enjoyed by others throughout the country and the world. Multicultural education is a requirement, we all live in a multicultural, multi-faith nation and world.

We ave tried to balance traditional Christian and secular celebrations, some of which have roots in pagan times, with cultural and religious celebrations from faiths around the world. We have concentrated on those which are more accessible to the youngest children in our care, who are just beginning to recognise similarities and differences between their own lives and those of the children and adults they meet.

At the back of the book we identify some resources and some web sites where you can find more information about the background to the activities or the festivals of other faiths.

Using the book

There is no need to follow the book in the order it is presented! The activities are loosely grouped in seasons, starting with the autumn, so you can follow the activities throughout the year, dipping into the book, either for focus activities or those which you can integrate into seasonal or other themes.

Every page has:
* a short introduction to the celebration, including some background;
* resources you could collect, or that you need for the activities;
* some suggested vocabulary;
* specific goals for the Early Years Foundation curriculum;
* suggestions for preparation before you embark on the activity;
* step by step guidance for the main activity;
* other activities you may want to include as extension or enrichment.

Cross-curricular links

Celebrating special events and days gives us plenty of opportunity to learn about other people, but it is important to remember that children do not restrict their learning to the goals we identify! Of course, this book may be used to address those complex goals in PSED, but we must not forget that children make and take opportunities for learning across all areas of the curriculum, and will apply skills and knowledge learned in one activity to many others.

All the activities:
* are carefully planned to help children make progress towards the Goals;
* cover all six areas of learning;
* are practical and easy to do;
* have clear, concise instructions to follow;
* can easily be adapted for children at different developmental stages.

Through these activities, as with many others you plan, you are helping children:
* to be aware of a range of multicultural celebrations;
* to be tolerant of other peoples' beliefs;
* to recognise the varied rich cultures within our society;
* to be increasingly aware that different cultures have different celebrations that we can all share.

Remember to be sensitive to the needs and beliefs of the children within your setting. Some younger children may not fully understand the deeper ideas and beliefs that underlie the celebrations, but they will enjoy joining in with the activities, and enjoyment is key to beginning understanding!

> Some of the recipes in this book use eggs:
> Safety Advice on Using Eggs
> The advice to schools and settings is to use pasteurised eggs (either whole or separated) now available in supermarkets. Hard boiled eggs are quite safe for children to eat and to use in any recipe using cooked eggs.

Links with the Developmental Stages and Early Learning Goals

A small number of goals are identified on each activity page. However, there is a collection of over-arching goals relating to the celebration of faiths, views, feelings, thoughts and activities. These spread right across the Early Years Foundation Curriculum and appear in all six areas. A selection of these follows:

Personal, Social and Emotional Development
* Respond to significant experiences, showing a range of feelings when appropriate.
* Form good relationships with adults and peers.
* Work as part of a group or class, taking turns and sharing fairly.
* Understand that people have different needs, views, cultures and beliefs that need to be treated with respect.
* Understand that they can expect others to treat their needs, views, cultures and beliefs with respect.
* Understand what is right and wrong and why.
* Consider the consequences of their words and actions for themselves and others
* Have a developing awareness of their own needs, views and feelings and be sensitive to the needs, views and feelings of others.

Communication, language and literacy
* Interact with others, negotiating plans and activities and taking turns in conversation.
* Speak clearly and audibly with confidence and control.
* Use a pencil and hold it effectively to form recognisable letters, most of which are correctly formed.
* Write their own names.
* Sustain attentive listening, responding to what they have heard by relevant comments, questions or actions.
* Extend their vocabulary, exploring the meanings and sounds of new words.
* Use talk to organise, sequence and clarify thinking, ideas feelings and events.
* Use language to imagine and recreate roles and experiences.

Problem Solving, Reasoning and Numeracy
* Say and use number names in order in familiar contexts.
* Count reliably up to 10 everyday objects.
* Recognise numerals 1 to 9.
* Use developing mathematical ideas and methods to solve practical problems.
* In practical activities and discussion begin to use the vocabulary involved in adding and subtracting.
* Use everyday words to describe position.

Knowledge and Understanding of the World
* Investigate objects and materials by using all their senses as appropriate.
* Look closely at similarities, differences, patterns and change.
* Ask questions about why things happen and how things work.
* Find about and identify the uses of everyday technology and use ICT to support their learning.
* Find out about past and present events in their own lives, and in those of their families and other people they know.
* Find out about and identify some features of living things, objects and events they observe.
* Begin to know about their own cultures and beliefs and those of other people.

Physical development
* Move with confidence, imagination and in safety.
* Move with control and co-ordination.
* Show an awareness of space, of themselves and others.
* Handle tools, objects, construction and malleable materials safely and with increasing control.

Creative Development
* Respond in a variety of ways to what they see hear, smell, touch and feel.
* Explore colour, texture, shape, form and space in two and three dimensions
* Use their imagination in art and design, music, dance, imaginative role play and stories.
* Recognise and explore how sounds can be changed, sing simple songs from memory, recognise repeated sounds and match movements to music.

Celebrations Calendar

This calendar does not attempt to include <u>all</u> significant dates, nor the celebrations of all faith groups. Further information can be obtained from the Internet or from individual faith groups,

January	1st	New years Day	Christian	Day for resolutions
	5th	Guru Gobind Singh	Sikh	
	7th	Haile Selaisse's Birthday	Rastafarian	
	14th	Makar Sankrant	Hindu	New beginnings
	▶	Epiphany	Christian	
	▶	Chinese New Year	Taoism	Dragons and lions
	▶	Mkar Sakranti	Hindu	Mid winter ▯ flying kites

February	5th	Lantern Festival	Chinese	
	14th	St Valentines Day	Christian	
	▶	Eid-ul-Adha	Muslim	Festival of sacrifice. Concludes the Hajj or visit to Mecca
	▶	Carnival/Mardi Gras	Brazil/USA	
	▶	Al Hijara (New Year)	Muslim	Migration of Mohammed & establishment of first Muslim state.
	▶	Shrove Tuesday	Christian	Beginning of Lent. Pancakes
	▶	Shiv Ratri	Hindu	Shiva celebrated with flowers
	▶	Ash Wednesday	Christian	Beginning of Lent

March	1st	St David's Day	Christian, Wales	Leeks and daffodils
	3rd	Ohina Matsuri	Japan	Girls festival or dolls' festival
	5th	Sri ram Krishna	Sikh	Birthday of Krishna
	17th	St Patrick's Day	Roman Catholic	Shamrock
	▶	Ashura	Muslim	1 day fast to recognise Creation & Noah's departure from the Ark
	▶	Holi	Hindu	Spring festival ▯ coloured water and red/green powder sprays
	▶	Sikh New Year	Sikh	
	▶	Mothering Sunday	Christian	

April	1st	April Fools Day	Christian	Jokes and tricks on your friends
	23rd	St George's Day	Christian, England	Defeat of the dragon of evil
	▶	Palm Sunday	Christian	Entry of Jesus into Jerusalem
	▶	Ancestral Day	Chinese	Festival of pure Brightness
	▶	Passover (8 days)	Jewish	Escape of the Jews from Egypt
	▶	Hana Matsuri	Buddhist	Flower festival for a good harvest
	▶	Good Friday	Christian	
	▶	Easter	Christian	Death of Christ. Eggs and Spring
	▶	Vaisakha/Baisakhi	Sikh/Hindu	Sikh commemoration of the Sikh brotherhood. Hindu Start of the year. Greetings & wishes of good luck

May	1st	May Day		Maypoles etc
	5th	Tango No Sekku	Japan	Boys festival
	▶	Birthday of Mohammed		Muslim
	▶	Wesak (Buddha Day)	Buddhist	Buddha's Birthday

The Little Book of Celebrations

June	1st Esakha Puja	Buddhist	Buddha day
	22nd Dragon Boat Festival	Taoism	
	▶ Shauvot (2 days)	Jewish	Moses descent with 10 commandments.
		Flowers and plants used in decoration	
	▶ Father's Day		USA/UK
July	23rd Personal birthday of	Haile Salassie	Rastafarian
	▶ Puja	Buddhist	Turning of the Wheel of Teaching.
	▶ Raksha Bandhan	Hindu	Brothers and sisters
	▶ Esala Perehera	Buddhist	Elephant parades
	▶ Obon	Japan	Feast of lights
August	17th Marcus Garvey	Rastafarian	Birthday
	▶ Lammas	Christian	First fruits of the harvest
September	11th New Years Day	Rastafarian	
	▶ Rosh Hashanah	Jewish	Jewish New Year
	18th Ganesh-Chaturthi	Hindu	Prosperity and success. Parvati breathed life into a doll of dough
	▶ Yom Kippur	Jewish	Day of Atonement; fast day
	29th Lailat al Baar'ah	Muslim	Forgiveness day
	▶ Sukkot (3 days)	Jewish	Jewish harvest festival
	▶ Harvest Festival In the northern hemisphere		
	▶ Moon Festival Taoist		
October	22nd Family day	Chinese	
	30th All Hallow's Eve	Christian (Halloween)	Prayers and merriment.
	▶ Navratri/Dusherah	Hindu	Nine day festival of the wife of Shiva and the days of Krishna
	▶ Dusherah	Hindu	Dancing festival to end Navrati
	▶ Ramadan	Muslim	Holiest period for Muslims, Fasting from sunrise to sunset
November	1st All Saints Day	Christian	Honouring of all saints
	11th Remembrance Day*	UK and WW2 allies	Remember those who died in the 2nd World War
	28th Birth of Guru Nanak	Sikh	Birthday of founder of Sikh faith
	30th St Andrew's Day	Christian Scotland	
	▶ Thanksgiving	USA	Celebration of the earth and food
	▶ Divali/Diwali	Hindu	Festival of Lights
	▶ Deepavali	Hindu	5 day festival, end of Hindu year
	▶ Bestu Varash	Hindu	New Year
	▶ Eid-ul-Fitr	Muslim	3 day fast marking end of Ramadan.
	▶ Advent	Christian	Preparation for the birth of Jesus
December	▶ Chanukah	Jewish	8 day Festival of Lights. Chanukiah lit
	21st Longest Night		
	22nd Harvest Festival	Chinese	
	25th Christmas	Christian	Birth of Christ
	Kwanzaa 26/12 to 1/01	African	Family, community, culture

▶ festivals where the date (and sometimes the month) changes according to the lunar or other calendar

* usually celebrated on the Sunday closest to November 11th

Who's New Round Here?
new babies and how we welcome them

New children will all need to settle in to a new class or setting. Inviting a new baby to visit is a good way to focus on being new by talking about how new babies behave and what they need to learn. You could also use the opportunity to talk about Christening and baptism.

What you need
* books about Christenings
* Christening gowns, cards, presents
* photographs of Christenings
* books and stories about babies from a variety of backgrounds, races and cultures

Key words
* birth
* Christening
* gown
* font
* celebration
* special
* gift
* godparents
* church
* name

Early learning goals
* Begin to know about their own cultures & beliefs & those of others. (KUW)
* Interact with others, negotiating plans & taking turns in conversation. (CLL)

What you do

Your preparation:
* Collect the books and resources you need. Ask around to see if you can find some Christening photos. Research a willing parent who can bring a baby to meet the children.

Before the baby comes to visit, and while they are with you:
1. Talk to the children about the things they want to know or ask.
2. Make sure the children know how to welcome visitors and about being polite and quiet around a young baby.
3. Talk about to the children about new baby celebrations and explain that a Christening is a Christian celebration of a child being born and welcomed into the Christian church.
4. Show the children some Christening photographs. The children could bring in photographs of their Christening, and photographs of when they were babies, so you can all look and talk about them. Children will also love talking about staff photos of when they were babies!
5. Look at the selection of books and artifacts used at Christenings. In small groups, let the children look at the different things and talk about how they are used and what they are called.
6. If you have a picture of a Christening in action, talk about the font and how the baby may feel when water is been put on its head. How do the children feel when they have water on their heads? Talk about baptisms where people get right into the water.
7. Offer the children an opportunity to have their own Christenings in your setting, using dolls from the home corner.

And another idea......

* Visit different places of worship to see how babies in other cultures are welcomed into the world.
* Have a 'Guess the Baby' competition with photos. Can you guess who the babies are?
* Tell lots of baby stories and talk about all the things the children have learned to do.

The Little Book of Celebrations

Lanterns for Full Moon
Zhong Qui - the Chinese Mooncake Festival

In September, Chinese Confucians celebrate the birthday of Confucius, the founder of the their religion. Mooncake Day is a festival for the Moon Goddess. It is celebrated in September or October, depending on the lunar calendar, by making lanterns and eating moon cakes.

What you need
* small glass jars
* thin card, tissue and cellophane paper in several colours
* scissors, string or ribbon, glue
* tea lights or night lights
* clean dry sand

Key words
* celebrate
* lanterns
* full moon
* goddess
* festival
* China
* parade
* dark
* night

Autumn

Early learning goals
* Begin to know about their own cultures & beliefs & those of others. (KUW)
* Handle tools, objects, construction and malleable materials safely and with increasing control. (PD)

What you do

Your preparation:
* Collect the books and resources you need. Check safety issues of candles and matches. Find some books about night and the dark. Look for pictures of different sorts of lanterns (try garden centre catalogues or gardening magazines).

Introducing the celebration and doing the activity:
1. Gather the children in a quiet area. Tell them about the Chinese Moon Festival that is celebrated in the Far East when the full moon is at its brightest. People make moon cakes and special lanterns are lit to mark the celebration.
2. Look at some pictures of lanterns and talk about the different styles and shapes. Explain to them how they can make their own Chinese style lanterns using the jars and coloured paper.
3. Show the children how they can make a concertina out of the coloured paper or card. Younger children could tear tissue paper or cellophane and stick it onto the outside of the jars. Help children with folding and cutting if they need it.
4. Carefully wrap the concertinas around the jam jar to create the lantern. Put a small amount of sand inside each jar and let each child place an unlit tea light inside their lantern.
5. Put the lanterns on a safe shelf or table, and light the tea lights. (ADULTS ONLY)
6. Watch with the children as the lanterns shine. Imagine how they would look as the Chinese children carry them in a procession.

And another idea......

* Collect objects which make or reflect light. Get the children to help you make a display.
* Take the lanterns outside and place them on the ground. Light the candles. Watch what the tea lights do when lit out of doors.
* Make some moon cakes (recipe at the end of this book)

Grandparents' Day
a party for grandparents

Many cultures celebrate their grandparents and ancestors at special festivals. Remember that today's grandparents will be younger than our stereotypes! Many will be working or will have full diaries, so give them plenty of notice if you want them all to come!

What you need
* card, pens and collage bits for invitations
* cups/saucers, tea, coffee, sugar
* fairy cakes, shortbread or other simple cakes that children can make themselves

Key words
* tea-party
* grandma
* grandad
* invitation
* special day
* baking
* chairs
* flowers
* decorations

Autumn

Early learning goals
* Sustain attentive listening, responding to what they have heard by relevant comments, questions or actions. (CLL)
* Speak clearly and audibly with confidence & control & show awareness of the listener, for example by their use of conventions such as 'Please' and 'Thank you.' (CLL)

What you do

Your preparation:
* Be sensitive to children's family circumstances as you plan, and plan your celebration well in advance, so you get plenty of grandparents at the party. You could do some of the cooking in advance and freeze it. Contact parents so they know what is going to happen and when.

Introducing the celebration and doing the activity:
1. Talk to the children about older people and specially about grandparents - what they do and how they help families. Encourage the children to talk about their grandparents and the things they love about them.
2. Now suggest to the children that they could plan a special tea party for a Grandparent's Day to say 'Thank you' for all the special things they have done.
3. Offer the children the materials to make invitations. Talk about what invitations look like and what they are for. You could print the date and place for the party on a computer label for younger children to stick on the invitation. Give children the option of inviting someone else they know if their grandparents can't come.
4. Plan what you need to do, and help the children to make the refreshments (you could decorate ready made biscuits if you can't make them). Organise tea, coffee and juice for the tea party. Don't forget flowers, decorations, folded napkins, doileys etc.
5. Remind the children of how to behave when visitors come - showing visitors to their chairs, talking to them, perhaps showing them some of their work.
6. Talk about what questions to ask, what the children want to know about, that grandparents might know.

And another idea......

* Invite grandparents to other events in your setting (parties, performances, gardening events, fund raising etc)
* Ask grandparents to lend photos, books or other mementoes for a display.

A Very Special Elephant
Ganesh Chaturthi, the elephant God

The Hindu God Ganesha is the god of wisdom and art, who appears with the head of an elephant. His trunk is said to remove obstacles to success, and Hindus think of him when they go on a journey, move house, or start a new business. His festival is in September.

What you need
* collage materials, boxes, tubes, card, string etc
* sticky tape, scissors, pens, paint
* reference books and pictures of elephants
* elephant stories

Key words
* Ganesh Chaturthi
* Ganesha
* Hindu
* elephant
* symbol
* statue
* good luck
* festival

Autumn

Early learning goals
* Explore colour, texture, shape, form, space in 2 and 3 dimensions. (CD)
* Begin to know about their own cultures and beliefs and those of other people. (KUW)

The Little Book of Celebrations

What you do

Your preparation:
* Collect the books and resources you need. You could collect some elephant ornaments and models and some pictures and books.

Introducing the celebration and doing the activity:
1. Explain to the children that Hindus believe the God Ganesha had the head of an elephant. This is because elephants can move things out of their way and can solve problems.
2. Talk to the children about elephants and what they look like. Think of words to describe elephants. Why do they think the Hindus use an elephant as a symbol of strength and good luck?
3. Explain that during this festival, Hindus celebrate Ganesh bringing them happiness and laughter. Talk with the children about what makes them happy and what makes them laugh.
4. Now suggest that the children can make their own elephant figure similar to the Hindu symbol. Show them the collection of materials and ask if they need anything else.
5. Help the children with their elephant design if they need it. Help them to join pieces of the elephant together. Encourage them to experiment with different materials.
6. When the elephants are ready, talk about how they made them and what they used.
7. Make a display of the elephants with photographs and books about the Hindu God, for the children to use for further ideas.

And another idea......

* Make a collection of elephant photographs, books, ornaments and toys to add to your display.
* Make a book of achievements, and add photos or pictures of children's achievements.
* Tell stories about elephants and find out elephant facts.
* Visit a temple to look for images and statues of Ganesha.

Harvest Festival
celebrate the harvest of food from around the world

There are harvest celebrations in many countries at different times of the year. The October festival is European and originated in ancient times when people thought the spirit of the corn was in the last sheaf and had to be protected over the winter.

What you need
* fruit and vegetables
* food items to give to others - these could be packets and tins as well as fresh produce

Key words
* harvest
* festival
* celebrate
* crops
* combine
* tractor
* fruit, corn
* vegetables
* gift
* thank you

Autumn

Early learning goals
* Respond to significant experiences, showing a range of feelings where appropriate. (PSED)
* Find out about and identify, some features of living things, objects and events they observe. (KUW)

The Little Book of Celebrations

What you do

Your preparation:
* You will probably need to co-ordinate this event with the rest of your organisation! Collect some seasonal vegetables and fruit for the children to explore, taste and smell.

Introducing the celebration and doing the activity:
1. Talk about Harvest Festival with the children. Explain that Harvest Festival celebrates the time when the crops are gathered ready for us to eat, and people say thank you for all the good food.
2. Look at the different fruit and vegetables and talk about how it grows, how it is prepared and where it has come from.
3. Explain to the children that many people give food at this time to people who are poor, or are elderly and can't get out easily to get food themselves.
4. Talk and think about what it feels like to have no money or no food.
5. How do the children feel when someone kind gives them something?
6. Organise a Harvest collection in your setting and take the food with the children to the local church. Or make a collection of money for people in other countries who are hungry. Explain to the children why you can't send fresh food to them.
7. Talk about how it feels to do something for someone else.

And another idea......

* Look at some of the fruit and vegetables and let the children cut them open to see what they look like inside. Smell and even taste some!
* Make special baskets and hampers which the children can decorate themselves to put the fruit and vegetables in.
* Do printing using cut up fruit and vegetables. (Push a fork into halved fruit and vegetables to make them easier to hold and dip in the paint).

The Little Book of Celebrations

Firework Frenzy!
create chalk pictures outside to celebrate

These days, fireworks are much more frequently used to celebrate special occasions, but the magic of fireworks never fades! Give the children a chance to work on a big scale in this activity, which might be better done after the November 5th day itself.

What you need
* big coloured playground chalk
* small hand sprays filled with diluted paint or food colouring
* big sheets or rolls of paper, blackboards or space on paths etc
* photographs of fireworks

Key words
* Bonfire Night
* Guy Fawkes
* Parliament
* bonfire
* fireworks
* sparkle
* whoosh
* colours
* danger
* fire

Autumn

Early learning goals
* Use their imagination in art, design, music, dance, imaginative role play and stories. (CD)
* Explore colour, texture, shape, form and space in 2 and 3 dimensions. (CD)

The Little Book of Celebrations

What you do

Your preparation:
* Collect some big sheets of paper, plastic, card, sides of big cartons, boards, etc. Or check the protocols in your setting about drawing on paths, playgrounds and walls.

Introducing the celebration and doing the activity:
1. Sit with the children and talk about Bonfire Night. Explain to the children that people light bonfires on this night to remember Guy Fawkes. Ask the children if they know who Guy Fawkes is.
2. Tell the children how he tried to blow up the Houses of Parliament a long time ago in 1605. This is why we use fireworks to remember him on the 5th of November each year.
3. Talk about fireworks. Think about the sounds that different fireworks make. Try making some firework movements or a firework dance.
4. Ask the children why fireworks are dangerous and talk about how to stay safe on Bonfire Night. Talk about people and animals that may be afraid of the fireworks because of the noises they make. Talk about how can you look after your pets on Bonfire Night to keep them safe.
5. Put on your coats and go outside with the children to show them the materials and surfaces you have prepared for their pictures. Make sure the children are well covered to protect their clothes.
6. Talk about the different shapes of the fireworks and the different patterns they make in the sky. Let the children make firework pictures on the ground, walls or other surfaces you have prepared.

And another idea......

* Try making a huge picture all together, with adults joining in too!
* Make some Bonfire Night food such as jacket potatoes and let the children choose their own toppings.
* Offer some ribbon sticks or streamers to make firework movements outside.

The Little Book of Celebrations

The Bonfire Band
make a noise for Bonfire Night!

Bonfires and fireworks are features of many festivals and celebrations, and are often used to scare away bad spirits. Make your own band and celebrate the sounds of a November night. You could have a parade, dress up and march around to the sound of your band.

What you need
* percussion instruments (either bought or made by the children)
* plenty of space
* costumes, ribbon sticks, coloured scarves etc.
* pictures of parades and bands

Key words
* band
* instruments
* march
* play
* crash
* bang
* shake
* rattle
* music
* conductor

Autumn

Early learning goals
* Recognise and explore how sounds can be changed, sing simple songs from memory, recognise repeated sounds and sound patterns and match movements to music.(CD)

What you do

Your preparation:
* Gather some tubes, plastic bottles and pots, elastic bands, dried peas, lentils or gravel, short bits of broom handle, tape, paint etc for making instruments. Collect a basket of simple instruments, ribbon sticks, scarves, hats and simple costumes for the band.

Introducing the celebration and doing the activity:
1. Make some instruments - shakers, simple painted sticks, drums etc.
2. Go outside with the made and bought instruments in a large box.
3. Gather round the box and look at the different instruments inside. Talk about the children if they know the names of the instruments and how to play them.
4. Encourage the children to explore the different sounds the instruments make. Get the adults to join in too, choosing their own instruments and talking with the children about the sounds they make.
5. Now talk about making your own piece of firework music using the instruments. Talk about the different sounds fireworks make, as they are lit, as they are taking off and as they explode in the sky and come back to land.
6. Help the children to make their own piece of music to play in their Bonfire Band.
7. Practice the music and then perform it as you march around.

NB If you haven't got enough instruments, some children could use ribbon sticks or scarves.

And another idea......

* Make up a name for your band.
* Play your band for parents or other groups in your setting.
* Use a tape recorder to record the band so the children can listen to themselves.
* Use ribbons and streamers, or other props to help the children move in different ways to the music.

The Little Book of Celebrations

Wait for the New Moon
a Muslim festival for the end of Ramadan

During Ramadan, Muslim people fast from sunrise to sunset every day for a month. At the end of Ramadan, everyone waits for the new moon to rise so they can all have a celebration meal, wear their best clothes and say special prayers. This event is called Eid ul Fitr.

What you need
* a space to dance in
* simple instruments such as cymbals, tambourines, bells
* Eid cards if possible

Key words
* Eid ul Fitr
* Muslim
* Ramadan
* fasting
* celebrate
* sunrise
* sunset
* party
* moonrise

Autumn

Early learning goals
* Show awareness of space, of themselves and others. (PD)
* Move with control and co-ordination. (PD)
* Move with confidence, imagination and in safety. (PD)
* Begin to know about their own cultures and beliefs and those of other people. (KUW)

What you do

Your preparation:
* Find out from the Internet when Eid is due to be announced. It happens at different times every year depending on the phases of the moon. You may have to move this activity from year to year.

Introducing the celebration and doing the activity:
1. Gather the children in a quiet space and talk about sunset and sunrise. Explain that Muslim people celebrate Eid at the end of Ramadan. (Ramadan is a period of 30 days when everyone older then 12 goes withoutfood from sunrise to sunset.)
2. Explain that going without food is called fasting, that Muslim adults fast, but not Muslim children under 12. Ask the children how they would feel if they could not eat for a long time.
3. Now ask the children to find a space for a dance about sunrise and sunset, moon rise and moon set. Talk to them about how they can move different parts of their bodies as they rise and set.
4. Use a simple instrument such as a tambourine to help the children to experiment with different movements.
5. Older children could try working with a partner. Use your adult helpers to work with the children and talk about the movements and give them a chance to look at other children's movements.
6. Talk about how people must feel after such a long time of fasting. Think about all the different celebrations people have during the year. What do they do? What sort of things do they eat? What do they wear? What sort of music and dancing do they have?

And another idea......

* Make moon shapes using different parts of your bodies, including hands and fingers in the movements. You could start off being a full moon and then make a crescent shape.
* Invite members of the Muslim community to come into your setting and talk about Ramadan and Eid to the children.

The Little Book of Celebrations

Light the Lights
celebrating Indian festivals of light

In November, Diwali (or Divali) is celebrated in India, Pakistan and Asian communities throughout the world. Diwali is a festival of lights, when little lamps are lit everywhere, down paths, round doors and inside people's houses. Chapattis are a different food to try for a Diwali party.

What you need
* stories and books about Diwali
* chapatti ingredients (wholemeal flour, water, water)
* frying pan
* somewhere safe to cook
* yogurt

Key words
* Diwali/Divali
* festival
* lights
* chapattis
* Hindu
* Sikh
* celebration
* mix
* knead
* dough

Autumn

Early learning goals
* Handle tools and malleable materials with increasing control. (PD)
* Respond in a variety of ways to what they see, hear, smell, touch and feel. (CD)

What you do

Your preparation:
* Familiarise yourself with the story of Diwali and how lamps lines the path on the return of Rama and Sita. You also need to practise making chapattis if you haven't made them before. Prepare the ingredients and make sure you have a safe place to cook.

Introducing the celebration and doing the activity:
1. Sit with the children and talk about Diwali. Explain that this is a festival celebrated by Sikh and Hindu people each year. Tell them it is also called the festival of lights. Ask them why they think it is called the festival of lights?
2. Explain to the children that special food is made for Diwali parties, and one of these foods is a special type of bread called chapatti. Invite them to have a go at making their own chapatti.
3. Discuss what you need to do before you touch food. Make sure you have all washed your hands and rolled up your sleeves.
4. Look at the ingredients and talk about where they come from. Name each ingredient and talk about what they feel, smell and taste like.
5. Help the children to mix 150-200ml of cold water in a bowl with 225g of wholemeal flour. Talk about what the mixture looks like and take turns to knead it. Ask the children how it feels on their hands.
6. Make sure the dough is kneaded properly and help the children to divide it into small pieces.
7. Show the children how to roll the pieces of dough into a ball using their hands. Now pat the ball from one hand to other to flatten it out.
8. Now fry each chapattis in an <u>ungreased</u> frying pan. Do this very carefully to make sure they do not burn.
9. Take the chapattis out of the pan and wait for them to cool before you eat them. You could offer some plain yogurt to dip them in.

And another idea......

* Taste different breads from around the world. Look at similarities and differences
* Make your own bread with the children and eat it with different toppings.

The Little Book of Celebrations

Light the Candles
another festival of lights

Long ago some people did not want the Jewish people to keep their religion so there was a big battle. When the Jewish people got back into the Temple in Jerusalem, the everlasting light was not burning. They only found enough pure olive oil for 1 day but it lasted for 8, until they could get more.

What you need
* a picture or a real chanukiah (the nine branched candle stick)
* construction materials including card tubes and flat bases
* glue, card, pens and crayons
* eight candles

Key words
* Chanukah
* Celebrate
* Festival of lights
* Jewish
* Chanukiah
* flame
* candle

Winter

Early learning goals
* Understand that people have different needs, views, cultures and beliefs that need to be treated with respect. (PSED)
* Recognise numerals 1-9. (PSRN)
* Say and use number names in order in familiar contexts. (PSRN)

What you do

Your preparation:
* Find a picture or a real Chanukiah (if you can't get hold of a Chanukiah, draw one so the children can see what it looks like). Get 9 candles and some number cards 1-9.

Introducing the celebration and doing the activity:
1. Explain to the children that Hanukkah is celebrated by Jewish people and is a festival of lights, where Jewish people light eight candles on a special candlestick called the Menorah. Tell them how the celebration of Hanukkah lasts for eight days to commemorate the eight days that the little lamp burned in the Temple in Jerusalem. It is traditional to give Chanukah gelt (money) and eat food fried in oil eg latkes (pototo pan cakes) and doughuts.
2. Older children could talk about freedom and liberty, which Jewish people also celebrate at this time.
3. Look at numbers 1 to 8 and work on recognising these with the children. Practice counting to eight using the candles or other objects.
4. Look at the pictures or the Menorah together.
5. Now suggest that the children could make their own Menorah using construction materials. Remind them to include eight candles, so a new candle can be lit each day of the celebration. They could make 2D pictures or 3D models.
6. Make eight flames for each menorah, one for each day of the celebration, and during the festival of Hanukkah help the children to put one flame on the menorah each day. Use the opportunity to count how many candles are lit and how many are unlit.
7. Display the Chanukiah collages or models in your setting.

And another idea......
* Look at a selection of different candles and compare them.
* Look at different fragranced candles and allow the children to smell them unlit. Can they guess what fragrance they are?
* Carefully light the candles with the children and smell them when lit.

The Little Book of Celebrations

Waiting, waiting, waiting
waiting for Saint Nicholas

Saint Nicholas is a Christian saint, whose day is celebrated on 6th December. Dutch children in the Netherlands expect a visit on this day, and they leave their shoes out for him to fill with presents. Children in North America, Britain and many other countries call him Santa Claus!

What you need
* books about Father Christmas
* a Christmas stocking
* pens, paper etc for letters
* big sheets of paper and big felt pens for map making
* small pieces of card for houses

Key words
* map
* route
* Santa Claus
* Father Christmas
* Christmas Eve
* house
* chimney
* stocking

Winter

Early learning goals
* Use everyday words to describe position. (PSRN)
* Use talk to organise, sequence and clarify thinking, ideas, feelings and events. (CLL)

The Little Book of Celebrations

What you do

Your preparation:
* Make a collection of books, cards, stockings etc to look at. Locate a local map for the children to use when they make their own maps.

Introducing the celebration and doing the activity:
1. Gather the children together to talk about the excitement of Christmas and Santa/Father Christmas visiting their homes.
2. Ask them how he knows where the children live. What could he use to help him find their houses?
3. Explain to them that they are going to make a big map and put all their houses on it. Look at the local map and talk about familiar places such as parks, shops etc.
4. Ask the children if they know where they live and help them to locate their home on the map.
5. On small pieces of cut out card, ask the children to draw the outside of their homes using the felt tips and crayons. Help the children to write their names and stick them underneath their houses.
6. Now stick the houses onto the big piece of paper to make a map for Santa. Say that you can send the map to the North Pole, so Santa knows the way when he visits on Christmas Eve.
7. Help them roll the large map up into a scroll and tie it with a ribbon. Write the address (Santa at the North Pole) on the scroll and let the children take it to the Post Office. Ask them first so they know!
8. Or you could leave the map outside with some reindeer food so the reindeer can find it and take it to the North Pole for you.

And another idea......
* Invite Santa to visit your setting to talk to the children! Make him some mince pies to taste.
* Offer writing materials and a post box so the children can make Christmas lists and letters to Father Christmas.
* Make your role play corner into Santa's Grotto.

The Special Baby
the Christian celebration of Christmas

The Christmas story is familiar to many children, but in a multicultural society, we need to balance the celebrations of many faiths, and may need to introduce children from other faiths to the traditional religious celebrations of this country.

What you need
* Christmas story books
* simple costumes and props for an informal telling of the story
* Christmas cards with Nativity pictures

Key words
* Nativity
* Christian
* Jesus
* stable
* story
* shepherds
* wise men
* Mary
* Joseph
* manger

Winter

Early learning goals
* Use language to imagine and recreate roles and experiences. (CLL)
* Speak clearly and audibly with confidence and control and show awareness of the listener. (CLL)

What you do

Your preparation:
* Collect the resources you need. You don't need a full set of nativity costumes - a baby doll, a box for a manger, and some simple lengths of cloth fixed with clothes pegs can make a really good experience!

Introducing the celebration and doing the activity:
1. Gather the children together to share the Nativity story. Explain that this is a Christian story to celebrate the birth of Jesus.
2. Talk about what a stable is and why there was no room for Mary and Joseph any where else in Bethlehem. Talk about the different animals that were in the stable and the different people who visit baby Jesus. Ask the children why they think these people came to see the new baby.
3. Look at the props you need to act out the Nativity story. Decide who is going to be each character - people and animals. If you have time, the children could make their own costumes, props or masks. Otherwise, let children choose what to wear from your 'prop box'.
4. Wrap up a doll as baby Jesus. Let them practice carrying it safely and rocking it gently.
5. Now help the children to tell the Nativity story, taking different parts. Let the children use their own words to tell the story or you could tell the story as they become the characters.
6. Talk about how we celebrate Christmas today and how different countries round the world remember the Nativity story. Try to find some story book versions from different countries.

And another idea......

* Turn your role play area into a stable so everyone can have a turn at all the parts!
* Invite parents to come and watch the children's Christmas Story.
* Hold your own carol concert and invite elderly members from your local community to come and watch.

New Year Resolutions
a new take on target setting!

The beginning of the new year in January is traditionally a time for making plans for a better or different year to come. Help your children to begin a lifetime of target setting and sharing hopes and aspirations for personal and shared future during the coming year.

What you need
* a comfortable place to sit and talk
* a display board or a scrap book to record hopes and aspirations for the year
* a camera (not essential)

Key words
* New Year
* different
* resolution
* promise
* hope
* wish

Winter

Early learning goals
* Have a developing awareness of their own needs, views and feelings and be sensitive to the needs, views and feelings of others. (PSED)
* Form good relationships with adults and peers. (PSED)
* Consider the consequences of their words and actions for themselves and others. (PSED)

What you do

Your preparation:
* Prepare a space or a book for the children's resolutions. You may decide to use a flip chart or big piece of paper to record individual thoughts, or you could use a scrap book or album with or without photos, so the children can return to it during the year.

Introducing the celebration and doing the activity:
1. Explain that on the last day of December it is New Year's Eve and that this is a special night, when everyone celebrates the end of the old year and welcomes in the New Year on the first day of January.
2. Now talk about New Year's resolutions. Explain that a resolution is like a promise what people make about something they want to do or change in the New Year.
3. Ask them why they think people make promises, then ask the children if they have ever made a promise. Have any of them broken a promise? What does it feel like if you break a promise?
4. Now you could start by asking the adults to make a New Year resolution so the children get an idea of what to say, then ask the children if they would like to make a resolution. Write down the things they say, and read them back to ensure you have got it right!
5. You could display these around your setting to help everyone keep their promises by working together as a team, or you could make a book with a photo of each child or adult next to their resolution.
6. A good listening end responding activity is to get children to tell each other their resolutions.

And another idea......

* Make a promise box with the children so they can post promises in the box.
* Practice counting from 10-0 with the children, then shouting 'HAPPY NEW YEAR!'
* Teach the children 'Auld Lang Syne', crossing their arms in a circle while they sing the song.

The Little Book of Celebrations

A Lucky Message in a Bag
a Chinese New Year custom

Chinese New Year is celebrated on the first day of the first lunar month (the end of January or the beginning of February). One tradition is that children are given Lucky Money in red paper bags or envelopes called Ang Pow. Red is a lucky colour for Chinese people.

What you need
* red paper and card
* ribbons, string, cord
* glue, scissors (perhaps some 'fancy cut' scissors)
* pennies

Key words
* Ang pow
* money
* lucky bags
* celebrate
* gift
* Chinese New Year

Winter

Early learning goals
* Use mathematical ideas & methods to solve problems. (PSRN)
* Use everyday words to describe position. (PSRN)
* Use language such as circle or bigger to describe the shape and size of solid and flat shapes. (PSRN)

What you do

Your preparation:
* Prepare the Ang Pow making table with scissors, paper etc. Make some sample Ang Pows to show the children how they could be made.

Introducing the celebration and doing the activity:
1. Gather the children in a quiet area and explain to them that it is the Chinese New Year. Tell them that this is a very important celebration for Chinese people.
2. Explain to the children that Ang Pows are given to children at New Year. An Ang Pow is a lucky bag which has money inside it. Explain that red is a lucky colour, so the bags are made from red paper.
3. Show the children the different ways they could make the bags. Look at the different pieces of paper and card on the table.
4. Suggest they could make their own lucky bags from different shapes. Encourage them to experiment with different sizes, shapes and types of bags and fastenings. Talk to them about the different shapes they can make by folding the card and paper in different ways.
5. Now give each child a penny. Let them put the penny inside their bag, to bring them good luck for the New Year. Discuss different ways of tying and fastening the lucky bags.
6. When the bags are finished, the children could show each other the different ways they have made their bags. Then they can take them home to give to someone who lives with them, or they could give them to a friend.

And another idea……

* Look at the different animal names for the Chinese years. Find out which year they were born in and which year you are in now.
* Look at different things from China, such as Chinese teas. You could show the children how to make and taste a cup of tea made with tea leaves.

The Little Book of Celebrations

Dancing Dragons
a Chinese New Year dance

Dragons and lions are specially lucky for Chinese people. At Chinese New Year, the dragons and lions dance through the streets, while the people make a great noise with drums and fireworks to scare away bad luck. Make your own dragon or lion costume for a dance.

What you need
* books about Chinese New Year
* coloured paper, streamers, ribbons
* boxes to make the head of the dragon or lion
* a large piece of fabric for the body
* percussion instruments

Key words
* lion
* dragon
* dance
* masks
* head
* body
* noise
* lucky
* music
* people

Winter

Early learning goals
* Respond in a variety of ways to what they see, hear, smell, touch & feel. (CD)
* Use their imagination in art and design, music, dance, imaginative role play and stories. (CD)

The Little Book of Celebrations

What you do

Your preparation:
* Collect the materials you need to make the dragon or lion costume. Find some pictures to help them when they are making the costume.

Introducing the celebration and doing the activity:
1. Tell a story or look at a book to help the children understand about Chinese New Year dances and processions. You could also play some Chinese music.
2. Talk about celebrating the New Year by having street parades. Ask the children if they have seen a street parade and what happens.
3. Help the children to design and make their own lion or dragon masks so they can make their own parade. They could each make their own or work with friends. Or you could make a gigantic head and a body of fabric that fits the whole group.
4. Talk about the different materials and equipment they might need to make the heads or masks. Look at books and pictures of the Chinese New Year so the children can look at the shapes and colours. Help them if they need it.
5. When the heads are dry, talk about different ways they could move wearing their masks. Practice different movements.
6. Offer the children some instruments to accompany their dance. Experiment with different sounds.
7. Put on a parade in your garden or playground to celebrate the Chinese New Year with a lion or dragon dance and suitably noisy music to scare away bad luck. Invite other children in your setting to watch.

And another idea......

* Make decorations to display around your setting and garden for the celebration.
* Invite parents and other members of the community to come and get involved in the celebrations.
* Try eating noodles or rice with chopsticks.

The Little Book of Celebrations

Mix a Pancake
Pancake day is a good opportunity for some cooking

Pancake Day/Shrove Tuesday (also called Mardi Gras) is celebrated on the last day before Lent begins on Ash Wednesday. Lent is a time when Christian people think about Jesus and eat very simple food. On Pancake Tuesday people eat up all the rich foods left before Lent.

What you need
* fork, bowl, frying pan, oil, fish slice
* flour, eggs, milk
* lemon juice and sugar, or jam, banana slices, honey, grated cheese etc for fillings
* The Enormous Pancake story

Key words
* Shrove Tuesday
* Lent
* pancake
* celebrate
* mix
* batter
* toss/turn
* filling
* favourite

Spring

Safety Advice on using eggs (page 5)

Early learning goals
* Investigate objects & materials by using all their senses. (KUW)
* Explore colour, texture, shape, form and space in two or three dimensions. (CD)

What you do

Your preparation:
* Collect the resources you need. Make sure you have a safe place to cook and eat the pancakes.

Introducing the celebration and doing the activity:
1. Talk to the children about Shrove Tuesday and why it is a special celebration. Explain that it is the day before Lent and that pancakes were made so all the eggs and fat in the cupboards were used up, ready for the fasting of Lent.
2. Talk about pancakes. Ask the children if they know how they are made. What ingredients do the children think they will need?
3. Wash your hands before you touch the ingredients.
4. Look at the ingredients with the children. Do the children know what each ingredient is? Look at, smell and touch the ingredients.
5. Now make the pancake mix: (*Makes 10 medium size pancakes*)
   200/8oz self-raising flour (sifted)   knob of melted butter
   1 egg   drop of sunflower oil
   1tsp baking powder   a selection of fillings
   300ml/half a pint milk
6. Measure out the ingredients with the children.
7. Mix the flour and baking powder in a large bowl carefully.
8. In a jug beat the egg and the milk together with a fork.
9. Make a small well in the flour mixture and pour in the milk gently, mixing to make a smooth batter. Add the melted butter and mix again.
10. Heat the oil in the frying pan and drop in a tablespoon of batter per pancake. You should be able to fit about four smaller pancakes into the pan at a time.
11. On a medium heat, cook the pancakes for around 3 minutes. Flip them over and give them another 3 minutes until golden.
12. Put on a plate and let the children choose their own fillings.

And another idea......

* Tell the Pancake story.
* Have a pancake party with a Pancake Race. Invite parents and community friends to join in.

The Little Book of Celebrations

Oh Let's Have a Carnival

have a carnival parade at almost any time of year

Whether they are called Mardi Gras, Carnival, Mela or another name, street carnivals are celebrated in many countries. They are particularly lively in the Caribbean, in South America and in Mediterranean countries. There is also a huge annual Carnival in London.

What you need

* carnival pictures and posters
* brightly coloured fabrics, ribbons, streamers, tissue and crepe paper
* coloured string and thread
* needles, safety pins, pegs
* pens, paint, glue, crayons

Key words

* carnival
* parade
* music
* masks
* costumes
* floats
* band
* instruments
* decorate
* noisy

Spring

Early learning goals

* Explore colour, texture, shape, form and space in 2 and 3 dimensions. (CD)
* Use their imagination in art and design, music, dance, imaginative role play and stories. (CD)

What you do

Your preparation:
* Look for some pictures of carnivals and street processions. Collect the materials you need for costumes, masks and head dresses.

Introducing the celebration and doing the activity:
1. Explain to the children that carnivals are happy times, where every one comes together and has a big party, often in the streets. Ask the children if they can remember when they went to a party and how they felt.
2. Show them how they can make a carnival mask to wear at the parade. Pre-cut eyeholes in different shaped strips of paper or paper plates, and let the children decorate them as they choose. Offer short sticks if children do not wish to wear them on their faces.
3. Suggest that the children could create their own carnival costumes to go with their masks. Look at a selection of the different fabrics. Talk about how they can make their costume, by wrapping it around their body.
4. Help the children to sew, pin or peg chosen pieces of the material onto themselves or each other. Talk to the children about how the carnival costumes could be fastened and have a practice with the masks too.
5. Explain that at the carnivals they sometimes have floats to carry people through the street parties. Put some chairs in a line, decorate them with strips of brightly coloured crepe paper and different fabrics. Sit on the float in your costumes and wave to the crowds!

And another idea......

* Make some carnival music to dance to. Use a selection of instruments and body percussion such as clapping, tapping knees and clicking to get into the carnival mood!
* Use large boxes to make a moving float for use outside.
* Make flags to wave at the carnival street parade.

The Little Book of Celebrations

Spray Day!
celebrate Holi with a spray day

Holi is the Hindu festival of Fire and of the Spring wheat harvest. Holi is celebrated in February or March (check a website calendar for the date each year). It's a festival of bonfires, loud noises, dancing and fireworks, and people spray each other with red powder and coloured water.

What you need
* waterproof clothing
* hand sprays
* food colouring or thin paint
* wellies
* big sheets of paper, old sheets, cheap shower curtains

Key words
* celebration
* Holi
* Hindu
* spring
* harvest
* joke
* spray
* paint
* colouring
* friends

Spring

Early learning goals
* Ask questions about why things happen and how things work. (KUW)
* Look closely at similarities, differences, patterns and change. (KUW)

What you do

Your preparation:
* Make sure children have waterproof clothes and footwear. The activity involves spraying on paper, sheets or plastic, but sometimes the sprays get out of control!
* Pin up some sheets or big pieces of paper outside.

Introducing the celebration and doing the activity:
1. Talk to the children about the festival of Holi and tell them about the people spraying each other with red powder and coloured water.
2. Ask them if they would like to do some spraying on paper, not people!
3. Let the children help to make up the spray bottles of water and colouring or paint. Watch what happens as the colour mixes with the water. The mixture should not be so strong that it will stain skin or clothes.
4. Make sure the children are warmly dressed and waterproofed!
5. Take the coloured sprays outside and put them on the ground.
6. Let the children spray the sheets with colour, watching to make sure they don't spray other children.
7. When you have finished the activity, look at the sprayings and talk about what has happened to the colours.
8. If you are feeling brave, and the children are well covered you could let them spray clear water at each other in a run and chase game with children taking turns to be the sprayer.

And another idea......

* Gather a few dry ingredients such as sand, sugar, salt, gravy granules and mix these in water sprays. Talk about what happens now.
* Invite the children to create a special Holi picture using brightly coloured powder paints of yellow, orange and red. These are the traditional dyes used on this celebration.

The Little Book of Celebrations

My Mum is the Best!
celebrate Mother's Day

Mother's Day or Mothering Sunday is celebrated on the fourth Sunday in Lent (very late February or March depending when Easter is). On this day Christian villagers took gifts to their 'Mother Church'. Nowadays it is a family day when mothers are celebrated.

What you need
* books and pictures about mothers and children
* card, pens, glue, coloured paper, ribbon, sequins etc.
* a photograph of each child

Key words
* Mother/Mum
* special
* celebrate
* love
* card
* flowers
* gift
* Sunday
* family

Early learning goals
* Find out about and identify the uses of everyday technology and use ICT to support their learning. (KUW)
* Write their own names. (CLL)
* Use a pencil and hold it effectively to form recognisable letters, most of which are correctly formed. (CLL)

What you do

Your preparation:
* Get permission from parents to photograph their children, and remove the pictures from the computer when you have made the cards.

Introducing the celebration and doing the activity:
1. Explain to the children that you are going to talk about Mother's Day. Tell them that Mother's Day is also known as Mothering Sunday and it comes on the fourth Sunday in Lent when some people give cards and presents to their mothers. Show sensitivity to children's individual circumstances when you talk about Mother's Day.
2. Show the children the digital camera (or ordinary camera.) Explain that they are each going to have their photograph taken. Talk to the children about what their mum would like their photograph to be like. Do they think their mum would like a grumpy face on her card or a smiling face? Ask why they think their mum would like a photo.
3. Take the photographs of the children against a plain background. If you have a digital camera, preview the photograph taken on the screen and share it with the children.
4. Let the children to watch their photograph being printed.
5. Help the children to make a card, using the resources you have prepared. Try to let them be as independent as possible, but remind them to leave a big enough space for the photo.
6. Talk with each child about why their mum is special and the things she does for them. Help them to write a message inside the card and write their name. Help them to stick their photo on the card.

And another idea......

* Make little cup cakes with the children, so they can give them as a gift to their mum.
* Hold a coffee morning for mums when the children can perform songs and rhymes.
* Make a Mother's Day celebration book using the things the children said about their mums being special.

The Little Book of Celebrations

Spring into Springtime!
celebrate new birth with some springing lambs

In Northern countries, Spring begins in March. The first flowers appear, and young animals are born. The traditional spring animals are lambs, rabbits, chicks and baby birds. Welsh people celebrate St David's Day on March 1st by wearing daffodils or leeks.

What you need to make meringue sheep

* 2 egg whites
* a drop of vanilla essence
* half a teaspoon cream of tartar
* 4oz/ 100g caster sugar
* chocolate drops, chocolate flakes
* two large baking trays
* kitchen foil, whisks, bowls
* icing bag fitted with 1cm tip

Key words

* Spring
* new
* baby
* sheep
* lamb
* meringue
* egg whites
* whisk
* bowl
* fluffy

Safety Advice on using eggs (page 5)

Spring

Early learning goals

* Find out about and identify some features of living things, objects and events they observe. (KUW)
* Respond in a variety of ways to what they see, hear, smell, touch & feel. (CD)

The Little Book of Celebrations

What you do

Your preparation:
* Collect books and pictures of baby animals and spring flowers.
* Collect the ingredients you need for the lambs, making sure the eggs are pasteurised to avoid salmonella.

Introducing the celebration and doing the activity:
1. Encourage the children to talk about Spring time. What do they notice happening around them? Explain to them that in Spring animals and plants grow and many have their babies.
2. Talk about animals having babies and see if the children know the baby animals' names.
3. Explain to the children that they are going to make meringue sheep and lambs to celebrate the start of Spring time.
4. Wash your hands first. Do any of the children know why they should wash their hands before touching food?
5. Make sure that all the surfaces you need to use are clean.
6. Follow the recipe for meringue sheep and lambs:
   Pre-heat oven gas mark 2 300F/150C
   * Help the children to line the baking trays with foil.
   * Break the eggs and separate the whites.
   * Let the children beat the egg whites with a whisk.
   * Add two drops of vanilla essence and the cream of tartar and continue to whisk until the egg whites make soft peaks.
   * Take turns at adding the sugar and whisking it until you can make stiff peaks again.
   * Now help the children to half fill the icing bag with the mixture.
   * Help the children to squeeze the mixture into little circles on the foiled baking tray. Make another little circle to form the head of each sheep or lamb.
   * Continue until all the mixture is used.
   * Put one chocolate drop for the eye of the lambs and sheep.
   * Bake in the oven for 12 minutes until the meringue is golden.
   * Turn the oven off and leave the meringues in the oven for around 30 minutes.
   * Remove from the oven and let the children add the flakes for the legs.
   * Share the sheep and lambs and enjoy eating them!

Friends together
Baisakhi (Vaisakhi) celebrations

Baisakhi (Vaisakhi) is celebrated by Sikhs. It is a celebration of bravery and brotherhood and there are parades and fairs in local communities. Sikhs are remembering the bravery of five members of their faith who gave their lives to protect a Guru or teacher.

What you need
* a quiet area where you can talk
* photos of the community round your setting
* a photo book or a scrapbook
* books and stories about friends

Key words
* Sikh
* friend
* celebrate
* brave
* Baisakhi
* neighbours
* home
* family
* teacher
* guru

Spring

Early learning goals
* Understand that people have different needs, views, cultures and beliefs, which need to be treated with respect. (PSED)
* Understand that they can expect others to treat their needs, views, cultures and beliefs with respect. (PSED)

What you do

Your preparation:
* Find out the date of Baisakhi for the current year (it changes because it's linked to the lunar calendar). It will be around 13th April. Make sure you are familiar with the major features of the local community. Collect maps and photos of the area.

Introducing the celebration and doing the activity:
1. Explain to the children that the festival of Baisakhi is celebrated on the 13th or 14th of April and is a special celebration for the Sikh faith and community.
2. Talk with the children about the word community and ask them what it means to them. Talk about the community round your setting, who makes up the community where the children live. You could identify special people and places, and talk about any that the children have mentioned. These might be neighbours, friends or family.
3. Now begin to look at other key people that make up their community; people who work there, such as crossing wardens, police workers, shop assistants, church workers, doctors, health visitors etc.
4. Do the children know who works in their community? You could use a local map or some photos to talk about key people and places.
5. Talk about your setting, and how important it is to be part of a group, to feel you belong. Explore some situations that make children feel part of your setting, and occasions when they might feel left out, for example when friends won't let them play, when new children start. How could you all make everyone feel welcome?

And another idea......

* Hold a community day in your setting and invite members of the community to come and talk about where they live or work and what they do.
* Play team games with the children to give them a taste of what it feels like to work together and help each other in a team.

The Little Book of Celebrations

A Spring Celebration!
find out how Jewish people celebrate Passover

In Spring, Jewish people celebrate Passover, remembering the time when their people escaped from slavery in Egypt and they only had unleavened bread (baked with no yeast) to eat on their journey. The eight day festival usually takes place in April, and emphasises freedom.

What you need
* pictures or stories of the flight of the Jews from Egypt
* horseradish root, parsley, salt, water,
* apples, nuts, grape juice, cinammon
* a grater and 2 bowls

Key words
* Passover (Pesach)
* Jewish
* slavery
* Egypt
* matza
* favourite
* taste
* like/dislike
* journey

Early learning goals
* Work as part of a group or class, taking turns and sharing fairly. (PSED)
* Begin to know about their own cultures and beliefs and those of other people. (KUW)
* Investigate objects & materials by using all their senses. (KUW)

What you do

Your preparation:
* Collect the books and resources you need. You could get some matza bread or other unleavened bread to try. If you can, find a seder plate (a Jewish ceremonial plate for the foods)

Introducing the celebration and doing the activity:
1. Gather the children in a circle in a quiet area.
2. Explain to them that they are going to talk about a Jewish festival that happens every year in the month of March or April.
3. Tell a simple version of the story of how the Jewish people were slaves in a place called Egypt, and how they escaped. Explain that Passover/Pesach is a festival which celebrates the journey of the Jewish people escaping from slavery.
4. Ask the children if they know what it means to be a slave. Explain that slaves were unhappy, they had to work very hard, and didn't get enough food and water. Ask them how the Jewish people would have felt when they escaped, and on the journey.
5. Explain to the children that Jewish people have a special Passover supper where the story of the Exodus is read and they eat special foods and drink 4 cups of wine to remind them what happened in the story.
6. Show the children the horseradish you have brought in. Let them smell it and taste it. It is bitter like the bitter time of slavery. It is eaten in a matza sandwich. They could try some if they like.
7. Make some salt water. Taste it and talk about the taste. Jewish people dip parsley into it to remind them of the tears that Jewish people shed when they were slaves in Egypt.
8. Make charoset by grating apple and mixing it with ground up nuts, cinnamon and grape juice into a paste. (You can use matza mea (ground matza) if you are concerned about nut allergies.) This is a reminder of the mortar used to make bricks for building the pyramids.

And another idea......

* You could sing this song to remind the chidlren of the work the Jewish slaves did when they helped to build the pyramids
  Dig, dig, dig goes my shovel deep, Dig, dig, dig goes my shovel deep
  For it's work, work, work every day and every night,
  For it's work, work, work when it's dark and when it's light.

The Little Book of Celebrations

Easter Egg Hunt
have fun in your garden with a simple egg hunt

Easter is a Christian festival , and it changes date from year to year according to the lunar calendar. Easter eggs have been symbols of Spring from ancient times, and have been adopted by Christians as an Easter symbol. They can be chocolate, wooden, or real eggs painted in patterns.

What you need
* some decorated eggs to look at
* foil covered mini eggs, a basket
* some clues in an envelope
* a template or sponge shape to make rabbit footprints

NB check the ingredients, some contain nuts!

Key words
* Easter
* chocolate
* eggs
* hide/find
* share
* clues
* collect
* Easter Bunny

Spring

Early learning goals
* Show an awareness of space, of themselves and others. (PD)
* Use developing mathematical ideas and methods to solve practical problems.(PSRN)

The Little Book of Celebrations

What you do

Your preparation:
* Find some pictures or examples of decorated eggs. Look for books and stories about Easter. Hide the little eggs in the garden and make some rabbit prints if you want to emphasise the Easter Bunny!

Introducing the celebration and doing the activity:
1. Gather the children together to talk about Easter celebrations. Ask them what Easter means to them. Young children may find the Christian Easter story frightening, so you may want to just talk about Jesus dying and concentrate on new life and Spring.
2. Talk about the ancient Easter egg tradition of Spring and new life and how this eventually turned into the tradition of giving chocolate eggs in some countries. Try to get some decorated eggs which are not chocolate, to show how different cultures celebrate.
3. Talk about the Easter Bunny, and tell the children that sometimes eggs are found in children's gardens.
4. Tell the children that they have had some post today and show them the clues in the envelope. Read the children the first clue that will suggest they should go outside to look for paw prints.
5. Help the children to work out the clues and follow the paw prints to find the eggs. Collect these in a basket (Remind the children not to eat the eggs as they find them!).
6. Make sure that there are enough eggs for each child and each adult helper in your setting.
7. Bring the eggs back inside and share them!

And another idea......

* Hard boil some eggs and let the children decorate them with paint or felt pens.
* Have an Easter egg race, rolling your eggs down a slope to see which one gets to the bottom first.
* Break open an egg with the children to see what it looks like inside.

May Time!

welcome the spring with your own May Day celebration

Dancing is a traditional way of celebrating the beginning of May. Maypoles, Morris dancing, ribbons, flowers and flags are all familiar signs of this day. In many countries, young girls are chosen as Queen of the May and they lead the processions and dancing.

What you need

* pictures, posters, books
* simple musical instruments, bells, tambourines, claves etc.
* ribbons, ribbon sticks, streamers
* a firm post to use as a Maypole
* flowers and leaves

Key words

* Maypole
* ribbons
* music
* flowers
* Spring
* May Day
* spring
* leaves
* celebrate
* dance

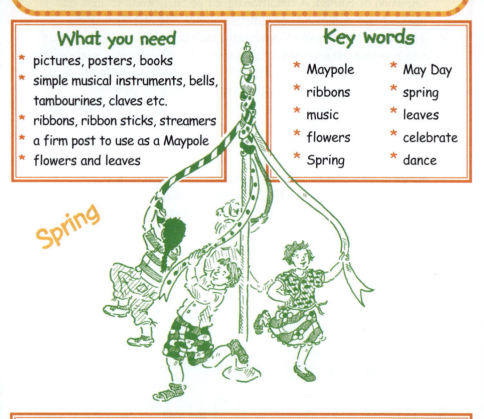

Spring

Early learning goals

* Use their imagination in art and design, music, dance, imaginative role play and stories. (CD)
* Recognise and explore how sounds can be changed, sing simple songs from memory, recognise repeated sounds and match movements to music. (CD)

What you do

Your preparation:
* If you are going to dance with ribbons joined to a Maypole, make sure it is firmly fixed in the ground. You could just dance round the pole waving the ribbons as you dance. Find some pictures of Morris and maypole dancing to help with ideas.

Introducing the celebration and doing the activity:
1. Talk about May Day, which is a celebration of the end of Winter and beginning of Spring. A traditional part of this celebration is doing a Maypole dance. Show the children a picture of Morris dancers and/or a maypole. Ask them what they can see and what they think is happening in the picture.
2. Show the children the instruments and let them experiment.
3. Let them use ribbons and instruments to move in different ways. They could practice travelling in different ways to show they are happy - skipping, leaping, jumping, bouncing, or twirling.
4. Now explain to the children that you are going to create your own May Day dance using the Maypole outside.
5. Help the children to decorate the Maypole with ribbons, flowers and leaves by wrapping or tying them around the post.
6. Make a circle together, around the post. Hold ribbons and instruments in your hands. Practice your happy movements, and join them together to make a group dance. Not all the children need to be doing the same movement. Give them the chance to experiment with movements they feel comfortable with.

And another idea......

* Invite parents to watch the children's May Day Dance in your garden.
* Try dancing with bells or ribbons tied round wrists and ankles.
* Take turns at being the May Queen or May King with crowns of flowers or leaves. Have a procession with the King and Queen at the front.

Feed the Birds
a Buddhist celebration

Buddhists celebrate the birth of Buddha at the full moon in April or May (check a calendar for the exact date). They cover the images of the Buddha with flowers and pour tea made from hydrangea leaves over his head in celebration of the Brotherhood of the Pure.

What you need
* books about eastern cultures
* a statue or model of the Buddha
* a blank book for a 'Friends Book'
* materials to make bird feeders
* bird food, nuts, seeds
* pictures of bird tables and baths

Key words
* Buddha
* Buddhist
* Wesak
* kindness
* friends
* flowers
* food
* help
* celebration
* birth/born

Spring

Early learning goals
* Understand what is right and wrong and why. (PSED)
* Consider the consequences of their words and actions for themselves and others. (PSED)
* Form good relationships with adults and peers. (PSED)

The Little Book of Celebrations

What you do

Your preparation:
* Collect the resources you need. A small Buddha statue would help.

Introducing the celebration and doing the activity:
1. Gather the children in a quiet area and explain that you are going to talk about a Buddhist celebration called Wesak. This is a celebration which remembers kindness to others and how Buddha taught others to be kind.
2. Talk to the children about what it means to be kind to others. Discuss the times that they have been kind to each other, drawing from examples from your setting. Can the children remember a time when they were kind at home?
3. Ask the children when others have been kind to them. What does it feel like when someone is kind to you?
4. Now talk with the children about how it feels when someone is unkind. Ask the adults to join in the discussion using their own examples.
5. Use a class puppet or doll to tell the children different scenarios as discussion starters, using situations familiar to the children.
6. Ask the children how they can be friends to living things, such as worms, ladybirds, caterpillars, spiders, birds.
7. Now help the children to make their own bird feeding area outside your setting and explain that by feeding the birds and providing water, the children are being kind and thoughtful.
8. Read some books about friendship and kindness.

And another idea......

* Make your own 'Friendship Book' and record some of the things the children do that are kind and caring. Share the book frequently with the other children to model kindness to others in your setting.
* Make kindness posters, showing photos or drawings of the children. Display these around your setting.

The Little Book of Celebrations

My Dad's Brilliant!
celebrate Father's Day with a party

Father's Day is a relatively new celebration, established to complement Mother's day. It is mainly celebrated in Western countries. Use this opportunity to talk about the things dads do and the special place they have in children's lives.

What you need
* materials to make cards, letters and invitations
* pictures of dads and grandads
* stories about children and their fathers
* a camera for the party

Key words
* Dad/Daddy
* Grandad
* family
* invitation
* celebration
* special
* love
* present
* card
* letter

Summer

Early learning goals
* Use talk to organise, sequence & clarify thinking, ideas, feelings & events.(CLL)
* Sustain attentive listening, responding to what they have heard by relevant comments, questions or actions. (CLL)
* Interact with others, negotiating plans & taking turns in conversation. (CLL)

The Little Book of Celebrations

What you do

Your preparation:
* Check to make sure that you are aware of family circumstances and that children don't feel left out. Collect stories about different sorts of families, including those with absent fathers.

Introducing the celebration and doing the activity:
1. Make sure that your invitations and posters are sent out in time to allow dads and grandads to make arrangements to come.
2. Have a discussion about Dads and how Father's Day is special because it gives people a chance to show how much we love others.
3. Help the children to make some cards or letters for Dads, Grandads, uncles etc. Be sensitive to children's family circumstances so everyone feels included. Other male members of the family could come to the party too.
4. Explain to the children that adults have dads too, as often children do not understand that grown ups have fathers! Encourage grandads to come to your setting with the children's dads.
5. Help the children to make the grandads and dads comfortable in the quiet area or outside. Have some drinks and biscuits for the children to hand round. Give the men the chance to talk to their own family members first before talking to others.
6. Ask them about to tell you all something about their family and the memories they have of the children.
7. Let the children give their cards and letters. The children could talk about what they have drawn or written. Take some photos!

And another idea......

* Make zig zag books with the children about the day and what they did.
* Let the dads and grandads play games with the children and join in with different activities inside and out.
* Make a book about the party, with captions from the children.

The Little Book of Celebrations

Stars and Stripes
celebrate the Fourth of July

The Fourth of July is a holiday in the USA. It celebrates the freedom of the United States from foreign rule. Many other countries also have Independence Day celebrations. Features of Independence days always include parades, music, flag waving and street parades.

What you need
* red, white and blue paint or chalk
* stars
* pictures and photos of parades and street parties
* string, sticks etc
* red, white and blue ribbons

Key words
* America
* Fourth of July
* independence
* flag
* parade
* pattern
* march
* band
* sing

Summer

Early learning goals
* Count reliably up to 10 everyday objects. (PSRN)
* Use developing mathematical ideas to solve practical problems. (PSRN)
* Talk about, recognise and recreate simple patterns. (PSRN)

The Little Book of Celebrations

What you do

Your preparation:
* Find some pictures of flags, specially the Stars and Stripes. Arrange a time when you can do a rather noisy parade outside. Invite parents in good time!

Introducing the celebration and doing the activity:
1. Gather the children in a quiet area and tell them that the Fourth of July is a holiday in the USA, which celebrates the country's independence. Families all have a holiday there are parades and parties everywhere.
2. Show the children the American flag and talk about the different colours and shapes they can see. Explain about the stars being for each of the states.
3. Make some Stars and Stripes flags. You could:
   * Make a big one on the ground with chalk.
   * Make small ones and hang them on strings indoors or outside.
   * Make individual flags on sticks.
   Give the children red, white and blue paint or chalk, and some examples of the Stars and Stripes flag for reference.
4. When all your flags are flying, Practice some music with simple instruments or find some marching music to play.
5. Make or find some hats and have a parade round your setting, garden or neighbourhood. If you give some notice, parents might be prepared to send their children in red, white and blue clothing, and join in themselves!

And another idea......

* Make red, white and blue bunting and have your own Fourth of July picnic outside.
* Help the children to think of different ways to hold their flag, by attaching straws, sticks etc.
* Help the children to make their own streamers from different materials.

The Little Book of Celebrations

Brides and Grooms
wedding ceremonies from all cultures

Weddings are celebrated in all cultures. Use this opportunity to help children understand that people are different, but we all have things in common. Look together at the way people celebrate weddings with different colours, activities, ceremonies, clothing, food and parties.

What you need
* books about weddings of all sorts
* wedding clothes, cards, confetti etc
* photographs of weddings
* party food and resources

Key words
* wedding
* ceremony
* celebration
* bride
* family
* friends
* party
* honeymoon
* promise
* present

Any season

Early learning goals
* Find out about past and present events in their own lives, and in those of their families and other people they know. (KUW)
* Respond to significant experiences, showing a range of feelings when appropriate. (PSED)

The Little Book of Celebrations

What you do

Your preparation:
* Send a note to all parents to ask if you can borrow wedding photos and other wedding things. Ensure they know great care will be taken of all their special things. Check that these represent all the cultures in your community. Ask colleagues and friends to help too.

Introducing the celebration and doing the activity:
1. Talk to the children about weddings, and why they think they are celebrated. Listen to their experiences.
2. Show the children the wedding photographs and see if they can sort them out into weddings that happened a long time ago and weddings that happened recently. Talk about the similarities and differences between the photographs.
3. Talk about pictures of weddings held in different countries and of different cultures.
4. Look at the different wedding artifacts with the children. What do the children think they were used for? Remind them to take care when handling other people's special things.
5. Ask different people from your setting or community to come and show the children items that they had on their wedding day and talk to them about their day.
6. Ask people to bring in their wedding costumes and do a fashion show for the children so they an see what the outfits look like on.
7. Ask the children to talk about who is invited to weddings and why they think they are such special occasions.
8. Look at the different foods we eat at weddings and try making and tasting some with the children.

And another idea......

* Make a wedding display.
* Make your home corner into a wedding place. Make sure you represent all cultures in clothing etc.
* Visit your local places of worship to find out about wedding ceremonies.

The Little Book of Celebrations

Happy Birthday to You!
think about birthdays, while waiting for yours

Children love making and looking at birthday cards, making parcels and having parties, even when it's nobody's birthday. This gives you a chance to talk about birthdays in general, and different sorts of parties and celebrations.

What you need
* birthday stories, old cards etc
* wrapping paper and gift boxes
* card, pens, envelopes for cards and invitations
* party hats, paper plates, pretend party food, streamers etc

Key words
* basket
* birthday
* celebrate
* years
* old
* present
* candles
* food
* games
* special

Any season

Early learning goals
* Respond to significant experiences, showing a range of feelings. (PSED)
* Have a developing awareness of their own needs, views and feelings and be sensitive to the needs, views and feelings of others. (PSED)

The Little Book of Celebrations

What you do

Your preparation:
* Collect cards, books, gift wrap, gift tags etc and put them in a Birthday treasure basket. Find some birthday stories. Make a list of adults' and children's birthdays.

Introducing the celebration and doing the activity:
1. Gather the children in a quiet place. Explain that you are going to talk about birthdays. Ask the children if they know when it is their birthday. Have a list to check for the children who are unsure.
2. Talk about what makes birthdays special. Can any children remember a special birthday that they had? What made that birthday special?
3. Ask the adults in your setting to contribute, talking about their birthdays.
4. Talk with the children about the special things used to celebrate birthdays. Make a list and a collection of birthday items. Ask the children to bring in old birthday cards, or other things they have received on their birthdays.
5. Children in your group may have very different birthdays from each other. Don't turn the activity into a competition or a time when some children feel inadequate or uncomfortable.
6. Show the children the birthday treasure basket you have started and encourage them to suggest or contribute other items.
7. Leave the basket where children can explore it and talk about the contents with others.
8. Encourage birthday play in the role play corner.

And another idea......

* Hold a birthday party for one of the soft toys from your setting. Take photographs of the different things that happen. Make these into a birthday book to add to the treasure basket.
* Play all sorts of party games with the children when you are outside.

The Little Book of Celebrations

A Place to Worship
finding and using resources in your community

Visiting local places of worship will give children opportunities to see faith and culture in action. Your local education authority (LEA) or RE centre should be able to give you information about the local places of worship and how to arrange visits for children.

What you need
* books and artifacts from different faith groups
* photos and posters of different faiths and in different languages
* videos of ceremonies
* a local map & a multi-faith calendar

Key words
* worship
* artifacts
* special
* celebrate
* faith
* building
* street
* belief
* country
* teach

Any season

Early learning goals
* Begin to know about their own cultures and beliefs and those of others.(KUW)
* Have a developing respect for their own cultures and beliefs and those of other people. (PSED)
* Respond to significant experiences, showing a range of feelings. (PSED)

The Little Book of Celebrations

What you do

Your preparation:
* Collect books and resources on as many faiths as you can, not just those represented in your setting. When you visit a church, temple or other place of worship yourself, ask if you can take photos and collect any leaflets, postcards or information available.

Introducing the celebration and doing the activity:
1. Invite people from different cultures to come to your celebrations days in traditional or religious dress. Display relevant artifacts and other resources on tables for the children to look at.
2. Visit local places of worship before deciding on whether a visit is appropriate and how long the children need to spend there. Talk to the people who know the place, and let them help you to decide on the sort of visit suitable for very young children. It's better to make several shorter visits than one long one when children may lose interest and concentration.
3. Don't forget local churches, chapels and halls where different Christian denominations worship and celebrate.
4. Make the visits and discussions part of everyday events such as local walks, shopping trips or other outings. Draw children's attention to places of worship as you would to other local features and buildings.
5. Encourage children to talk about the celebrations they have at home and with their families. Use scrapbooks and displays to follow the annual calendar of events for your community.

And another idea......

* Try making and tasting foods from different cultures, some of your visitors may be able to help make their own specialities!
* Never miss an opportunity to have a parade, wave some flags, sing and make music, but also remember the power of quiet thought and prayer.

Recipe for Moon Cakes (see page 12/13)

Children can make these cakes virtually unaided (except for the hot bit!).

For the dough, you need:
* 6 cups plain white flour
* 6 large eggs
* 3 cups sugar
* 750 grams butter or margarine
* a large mixing bowl
* a large wooden spoon
* a butter knife

For the filling, you need:
* jam, any flavour
* a teaspoon
* a board or clean table top
* a butter knife
* a flat baking tray
* baking parchment or foil to line the tray
* cling film
* a pastry brush
* a beaten egg for glazing

Safety Advice on using eggs (page 5)

What you do:
1. Cut up the butter/margarine into small blocks and put in the mixing bowl
2. Break the eggs, separating the whites and yolks. Put the yolks in the bowl with the butter/margarine and mix together.
3. Add the sugar and flour a spoonful at a time, stirring all the time. Soon the mixture will look like breadcrumbs. When this happens, you can use your hands to gather it together into a ball.
4. Wrap the ball of dough in cling film and put in the fridge for half an hour.
5. After half an hour, take the dough out of the fridge and unwrap it.
6. Break off pieces about the size of a walnut and roll into a ball in your hands. Sprinkle a little flour on your hands if the dough sticks to them.
7. Push a hole in the ball with your thumb.
8. Fill the hole with a small spoonful of jam, and gently squeeze the dough over the hole to seal the jam in (you can roll a small piece of dough for a little lid, but this is a bit fiddly for small fingers!).
9. Put the moon cakes on a lined baking tin.
10. Paint the tops with a little beaten egg to make them shine.
11. Bake in a hot oven for about 20 minutes until golden brown.
12. Cool well before eating - the jam gets very hot!

The Little Book of Celebrations

Some references used in the writing and editing of this book

* Feasts and Festivals; Jacqueline Dineen; Dragon Children's Books
* Illustrated Factopedia; Dorling Kindersley
* The Little Book of Persona Dolls; Featherstone Education Ltd

Celebrations Calendar constructed using:

* Interfaith Calendar *(Definition of Terms) May 2004:*
  www.interfaithcalendar.org
* Equalities Online Religious Festivals *(Sikh, Hindu, Muslim) April 2004:*
  www.birmingham.gov.uk
* Calendar of Religious Festivals 2004
* Cultural Festivals Calendar 2004: www.birmingham.gov.uk
* Religious Festivals 2004; *NASUWT:* www.teachersunion.org.uk
* Religious Festivals 2004; www.brent.gov.uk

Other resources

For books, try www.amazon.co.uk and search under either the festival of celebration, or multicultural books and stories.

Locally you could try:
  * your library service
  * a local multicultural centre
  * local places of worship

Don't forget that most early years suppliers will have multicultural items in their catalogues. These include:

dolls	puppets	Lego and Playmobil people
puzzles	books	child sized clothes
cooking implements		instruments

We also have a wide range of shops, market stalls and catalogues selling a range of cultural foods, clothes and artifacts.

If you have found this book useful you might also like ...

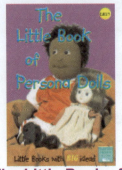

The Little Book of Persona Dolls
LB27
ISBN 1-904187-86-2

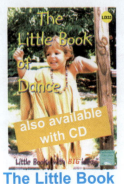

The Little Book of Dance
LB33
ISBN 1-904187-74-9

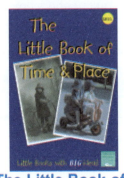

The Little Book of Time & Place
LB31
ISBN 1-904187-95-1

The Little Book of Christmas
LB5
ISBN 1-902233-64-6

All available from
**Macmillan Distribution Ltd
Howard Road, Eaton Socon
Cambridgeshire PE19 8ET**
T:01480 406625   F:01480 223131
on our web site
www.acblack.com
and from selected
book suppliers

The EYFS – Birth to Three

Little Baby Books offer lots of ideas for working with young children, and match the original birth to three framework.

A Strong Child   **A Skilful Communicator**   **A Competent Learner**   **A Healthy Child**

Set 1
978-1-905019-21-2

Set 2
978-1-905019-22-9

Set 3
978-1-905019-23-6

Set 4
978-1-905019-24-3

Also available with the activities grouped according to stage.

Book 1 Heads-up Lookers & Communicators (124pp)
978-1-905019-50-2

Book 2 Sitters, Standers & Explorers (156pp)
978-1-905019-51-9

Book 3 Movers, Shakers & Players (172pp)
978-1-905019-52-6

Book 4 Walkers, Talkers & Pretenders (238pp)
978-1-905019-53-3

All the activities in these books are suitable for the EYFS. Just look for the component and age you need.

To see the full range of Featherstone books visit
www.acblack.com

Continuity and progression

The **Baby & Beyond**™ series takes simple activities or resources and shows how they can be used with children at each of the EYFS development stages, from birth to 60+ months. Each double page spread covers one activity, so you can see the progression at a glance.

Shows how simple resources can be used by children at different ages and stages

Inspiration for planning continuous provision

Messy Play	978-1-905019-58-8
The Natural World	978-1-905019-57-1
The Sensory World	978-1-905019-60-1
Sound and Music	978-1-905019-59-5
Mark Making	978-1-905019-78-6
Construction	978-1-905019-77-9
Dolls & Soft Toys	978-1-905019-80-9
Bikes, Prams, Pushchairs	978-1-905019-76-2
Role Play	978-1-906029-02-9
Finger Play & Rhymes	978-1-906029-01-2
Dens & Shelters	978-1-906029-03-6
Food	978-1-906029-04-3

To see the full range of Featherstone books visit www.acblack.com

hrough the EYFS

Great for the Early Years Foundation Stage!

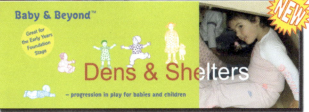

Ideal to support progression and extend learning.

Foundations Activity Packs

Ages 3–5

Each pack: • pbk, resources & CD £24.99 • 305 x 225 mm
• 48pp • colour photographs, black and white illustrations

These award-winning activity packs are bursting with resources – ideal for all adults working with children aged 3–5.

Written by Early Years practitioners and experts.

"Everything you need to plan, organise and lead activities on early years themes"
                                    Montessori International

The resources in each pack include:
- 50+ easy-to-follow activities
- 14 photocopiable activity sheets
- 8 colour photocards
- CD of poems, songs and stories
- Giant themed display poster
- Planning chart

Celebrations
Kate Tucker
9780713668452

Opposites
Rachel Sparks Linfield
9780713662191

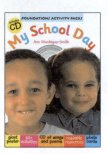

My School Day
Ann Montague-Smith
9780713661583

Minibeasts
Christine Moorcroft
9780713662184

Playsongs

9780713669404

Livelytime Playsongs
Sheena Roberts & Rachel Fuller
Early Years practitioner/parent resource:
• £9.99
• pbk (32pp) + CD

Baby's active day in songs and pictures.
A picture songbook which tells the story of a baby's day in glorious full colour and in songs with clearly described actions. Dances, peekaboo, finger and toeplays, teasers, knee bouncers and lullabies. **0–3 years**

Sleepytime Playsongs
Sheena Roberts & Rachel Fuller
Early Years practitioner/parent resource:
• £9.99
• pbk (32pp) + CD

9780713669411

Baby's restful day in songs and pictures.
A picture songbook and CD which tells the story of baby's restful day in glorious full colour and in songs with clearly described actions. **0–3 years**

Playsongs
Early Years/practitioner/parent resource:
• £12.99
• pbk (48pp) + CD

CD performances

9780713663716

72 songs and rhymes for babies and toddlers.
The perfect musical start for the very young – fully illustrated book and CD. **0–3 years**

To see our full range of books visit www.acblack.com